coolcareers.com

Software Designer

Alice B. McGinty

the rosen publishing group's
rosen central
new york

005.12
MCG

To my parents, Saul and Linda Blumenthal

The author would like to thank the following individuals for their valuable contributions to this book: Dave Blumenthal, Christopher Carlson, Mike Clark, Richard Coddington, H. George Friedman, Kevin Maxson, Brendan McGinty, and Robert Walker.

Published in 2000 by The Rosen Publishing Group, Inc.
29 East 21st Street, New York, NY 10010

Library of Congress Cataloging-in-Publication Data

McGinty, Alice B.
      Software Designer / Alice B. McGinty
        p. cm. — (Coolcareers.com)
      Includes bibliographical references.
      Summary: Explains what software designers do and how to prepare for a career in software design.
      ISBN 0-8239-3149-8 (lib. bdg.)
      1. Computer software—Development—Vocational guidance—Juvenile literature. [1. Computer software industry—Vocational guidance. 2. Vocational guidance.] I. Title. II. Series.
      QA76.76.D47 M397 2000
      005.1'2'0273 21—dc21

                                         99-043239

Manufactured in the United States of America

17.95

CONTENTS

About This Book 4

1. Computers: An Introduction 5

2. How Software Is Made 12

3. The Software Team 17

4. What It Takes to Be a
   Software Designer 23

5. Preparing for a Career in Software
   Design 28

6. The Workplace 36

Words.Com: Glossary 42

Resources.Com: Web Sites 43

Books.Com: For Further Reading . . 46

Index 47

ABOUT THIS BOOK

Technology is changing all the time. Just a few years ago, hardly anyone who wasn't a hardcore technogeek had heard of the Internet or the World Wide Web. Computers and modems were way slower and less powerful. If you said "dot com," no one would have any idea what you meant. Hard to imagine, isn't it?

It is also hard to imagine how much more change and growth is possible in the world of technology. People who work in the field are busy imagining, planning, and working toward the future, but even they can't be sure how computers and the Internet will look and function by the time you are ready to start your career. This book is intended to give you an idea of what is out there now so that you can think about what interests you and how to find out more about it.

One thing is clear: Computer-related occupations will continue to increase in number and variety. The demand for qualified workers in these extremely cool fields is increasing all the time. So if you want to get a head start on the competition, or if you just like to fool around with computers, read on!

chapter one

COMPUTERS: AN INTRODUCTION

A computer is only as smart as its software, the meticulous instructions, or programs, that tell it what to do and how to do it.

National Geographic, October, 1995

So, you're thinking about a career in computer software design. You've picked a good field! Software development is one of the fastest growing fields of the new millennium. If you look around you, this should come as no surprise. Computers play an exciting role in our lives. Not only do they give us games to play, but our cars, VCRs, and cellular phones wouldn't work without computers. Computers send satellites into space.

Businesses depend on computer software for record keeping, communications, and problem solving. Computers are involved in almost every aspect of our lives.

The widespread popularity of computers has created many jobs throughout our economy. Some people design and develop computer hardware. "Hardware" refers to the physical parts of the computer—anything you can actually touch. The computer console itself; its electronic parts, such as disk drives and circuit boards; the keyboard; the mouse; and the printer are all hardware.

Other people design and develop software; that is, the programs or instruction sets that tell the computer what to do. These instructions are called software because they have no physical parts. Even the medium that carries the instructions, the floppy disk or CD-ROM, is technically a piece of hardware. Software consists of human thought translated into electromagnetic impulses, and it cannot be felt or seen. Yet for every icon or window that you see on a computer screen, for every sound

the computer makes and every quantity it calculates, there are instructions or software programs telling it what to do.

As people develop better and faster computers, the need for better software follows. As people find more ways to use computers in their homes and businesses, more software is needed. The growth of the Internet and on-line communications also means that more software will be necessary. The number of jobs in the software field keeps on growing.

You probably have many questions about software design. What type of jobs are available? What kind of work would you do? What salary would you earn? What type of training and experience would you need? In this book, you'll hear from professionals working in the field of software design. They will talk about their jobs and help answer these questions and more.

There are also questions you can ask yourself. Do you like working on computers? What classes have you done well in and enjoyed in school? This book will tell you about the skills and talents that have helped software designers become successful. You can ask yourself if you have or could learn these skills too. By the end of the book, you will be closer to making an informed choice about whether a career in software design is right for you.

THE SOFTWARE INDUSTRY: PAST TO PRESENT ►►►►►►►►►►

Did you know that the word "calculate" comes from a Latin word that means "a small stone"? In early times, shepherds found that putting stones in a pot helped them to keep track of the number of animals in their herds. It was this need to collect and calculate information that led, step by step, to the modern computer.

One of the first machines people invented to help calculate numbers was the abacus. The abacus was invented over 5,000 years ago in China. Of course, this instrument could work no faster than human hands could move its beads. In the 1600s, Blaise Pascal invented a machine that used wheels and dials to add numbers. Later, Gottfried Wilhelm Leibniz invented the "Stepped Reckoner." It multiplied, divided, and found square roots as well.

In the 1700s, Charles Babbage designed a computer-like machine called the Analytical Engine. It could add, subtract, multiply, and divide. His friend Countess Ada Byron Lovelace, the daughter of the poet Lord Byron, wrote computer programs for Babbage's machine. The program

The abacus was the first counting machine.

instructions were in the form of punched cards, an idea borrowed from the French weaver Joseph Jacquard, who used such cards to control the patterns of fabrics produced by his looms. Unfortunately, only a part of Babbage's machine was ever actually built.

The American inventor Herman Hollerith (1860–1929), using the same system of holes punched into cards, built a computer-like machine to add up the 1890 census. You may have heard of the company Hollerith started. It is called IBM, the International Business Machines Corporation.

In the 1940s, the world's first electronic computer was invented. The ENIAC, the Electronic Numerical Integrator and Computer, weighed thirty tons and took up an entire thirty- by fifty-foot room. For switching devices, it depended upon thousands of vacuum tubes, which like lightbulbs would frequently burn out. In 1948 scientists at Bell Labs invented tiny switching devices called transistors. These replaced the large vacuum tubes and made computers much smaller. Transistors are made of solid materials and use much smaller electrical currents than vacuum tubes, so they don't burn out, making computers much more reliable.

People soon found many uses for computers. Today computers have revolutionized the way we work and play. New technology continues to make computers smaller and faster, and software has been written to help us in every aspect of our lives.

TODAY'S SOFTWARE INDUSTRY ▶▶▶▶

Today's software indus-try is huge. To help you understand it, let's break it down into cate-gories. There are two main types of software. The first is systems software. Systems

This is the operating software for the Apple Macintosh.

software works behind-the-scenes to control the basic opera-tions that all computers must perform, such as reading data from disks, controlling the onscreen display of information, organizing the storage of data on the hard drive, moving the cursor when the mouse is moved, and sending data to the printer. The most common examples of systems software are operating systems such as Windows or OS2.

The second type of software is called applications soft-ware. This is the software that you purchase and install on your computer to perform specific tasks. There are many types of applications software:

- Business software: These programs manage big jobs for private companies or governments. They handle accounting, sales, inventory, and payroll records, and sometimes they even control manufacturing processes.

- Office software: These are programs that help individuals work productively. Word processors such as Microsoft Word and spreadsheets such as Excel are examples.
- Educational software: These are programs that teach subjects or tasks, like reading, math, or science.
- Recreational software: These are the animated computer games that you may like to play.

Some software is sold in stores, designed for general use by thousands of customers. Other programs are custom made for people and businesses that need them for highly specialized jobs.

chapter two

HOW SOFTWARE IS MADE

Although there are many different kinds of software, the process of creating it involves the same basic steps. These steps are called the software life cycle. The process begins with an analysis of the problem to be solved.

NEEDS ANALYSIS ▶▶▶▶▶▶▶▶▶

The first step is to ask the following questions: Why is this software being created? What must it be able to do? What is the exact nature of the problem to be solved? The software designer must be able to put him- or herself inside the client's head and see the program from the user's point of view.

With custom made software, the designer works with clients to determine their needs. Mike Clark, president of Elmoco, is a consultant in the software industry. "When I do custom software development," he says, "I take the sketchy 'wants' of the client and create a specification." In a specification, the goals of the software are determined and described.

If the software is to be sold in stores, a marketing plan may be written. The marketing plan tells why the software is needed and who will buy it. It may seem premature to be working on a marketing plan before the software is even written, but by identifying whom the customers are, this plan tells the designer a lot about what the software must do and whom its features must be designed for.

Both marketing plans and custom software specifications describe how many workers and how much time and money it will take to develop the software. The client or corporation then looks at the plan. If it approves, the project moves ahead to step two.

DESIGNING THE SOFTWARE ▶▶▶▶▶▶▶▶▶

At the next stage, a "software design document" is created to show how the software will look and how it will work. "There are usually two parts to a design document," says Clark. "One is for the visual or physical look. The other is for the organization of the code."

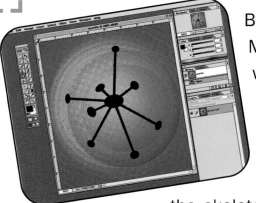

Brendan McGinty, president of Leo Media, is a consultant in the software industry. "When I design software," McGinty says, "I first try to lay out the whole program—what I want it to do and how I want it to work. I like to say that I design the skeleton first and then put the meat on the bones later."

Laying out plans for the text, pictures, and buttons that the user sees and interacts with is known as preparing the user interface design. "Almost every program starts with some kind of splash screen to introduce it," continues McGinty. "Then comes a menu to let you go where you want. Then for each screen, ask yourself what text, picture, sound, music, animation, and video would help to get your message across."

Kevin Maxson, chief technology officer and manager of system development for NovaNET Learning, talks about the importance of design. "In any project that more than one person will work on, the design is really critical. With a good software design document to work from, even junior developers can turn out a quality piece of software."

DEVELOPMENT AND IMPLEMENTATION ▶▶▶▶▶▶▶

During development, the software is put together by programmers following the outline of the design document. Sometimes authoring tools are used to put software together. Authoring tools are programs that allow software to be written by assembling pieces of preprogrammed code like building blocks. Text, pictures, and sound are added to make each program unique.

With more complex programs, much original code is written to tell the computer what to do. Maxson explains, "Once the software design is complete, implementation begins. Code is written, tested, and then reviewed by other developers."

TESTING AND VALIDATION ▶▶▶▶▶▶▶

Once the software is put together, it needs to be tested. "Bugs," or mistakes in the program, are found and fixed. Computer programmers spend a great deal of time debugging software, and if the problem is large enough, the designer will also be involved. The software must not only work, but it must be appealing in design and useful to purchasers.

Dave Blumenthal, a software engineer working with Hypercosm, talks about the testing stage: "I have to test my code and make sure that it works properly. I also work with others who test the software more rigorously than I can, trying it out on different types of computers."

Kevin Maxson explains, "Once we have a stable piece of software, we verify that it satisfies its goals. Then we pass it through a quality assurance cycle to catch any bugs or performance problems. After that, the software is released."

OPERATIONS AND MAINTENANCE ▸

If software is to be used over a long period of time, it has to be maintained. The people in charge of it continue to fix bugs that are found in the program. They add new features to the software and then market the revised program as an upgrade. They also improve the software so that it can run on new computers. With the development of faster and more powerful computers, software can perform more complex functions.

chapter three

THE SOFTWARE TEAM

Sometimes one person completes the software life cycle from beginning to end. More often, though, a team of people work together to create software. In this chapter, you will meet the people on the software team.

THE DESIGN TEAM ▶▶▶▶▶▶▶▶▶

"Large projects need many designers," says Mike Clark. "One designer might work with the user interface, which includes fonts, buttons, and screen layout. Another designer might work with transitions between screens, animations, backgrounds, and logos."

Frequently designers need help from other people. Experts in particular fields, known as content providers, help program designers ensure that the content, or information, in the program is accurate and complete. If the software is an educational program about jungle animals, an expert on those animals may be called upon to provide information for the program.

"One of the greatest bonuses of my job as a software designer is that I get to work in so many different fields," says Clark. "I don't have to be a doctor to work on a cancer treatment program, or a children's learning expert to work on a project about museums for kids."

Software designers also work with artists, or graphic designers. "If you aren't an artist, find a good one and have him or her add magic to your program," says Brendan McGinty. Artists help to create the special look of a program, and this may affect its ease of use and just how much people like to work with it.

If the software needs animation, the designer might work with an animation specialist. If it includes video, a videographer could help. These jobs all relate to the project. The software designer may perform some of those jobs or work with someone else who does them," McGinty says.

In educational software, instructional designers are used. Instructional designers have training in education; many are teachers. They determine learning objectives, or goals for the software. They design the software so that it teaches those objectives and then test to make sure that the user has learned them.

THE DEVELOPER, OR PROGRAMMER ▶▶▶▶▶▶▶▶

A developer, or computer programmer, puts together the software by writing code or using authoring tools. The programmer translates the designer's plans into specific instructions that the computer can understand and execute.

Writing code can be simple or complex for a programmer. In scientific, math, and engineering settings, programmers write code to solve problems using complex mathematical formulas. Programs for computer operating systems or animated video games with many levels of play consist of millions of lines of code. A good programmer can organize lengthy sets of instructions so that they not only work but work fast, and so that it is relatively easy to locate bugs when a program doesn't work. Good programming is almost an art form. Two programs written by different individuals may both do the job, but one may work seconds faster than the other because of the superior organization of its code.

In most large projects, teams of programmers each work on only a small segment of the complete program. These sections are called modules or units. The modules are put together later after each one has been perfected. Much of a programmer's time is spent testing and fixing (debugging) the program to make sure that it works.

Software designers and developers are sometimes called software engineers. This is most common in scientific, engineering, and some business settings. Designers who work on systems software, the behind-the-scenes software, are often called systems engineers, systems designers, or architects.

COMBINING DESIGN AND DEVELOPMENT ▶▶▶▶▶▶▶▶▶

Sometimes software is both designed and developed by one person. The use of authoring tools makes this easy for simple programs. For more complex programs, design and development are done by separate people. "Software design and software development can often be done by the same person for small projects," says Mike Clark. "For larger applications, there is just too much work for one person to do."

No matter how many people work on design and implementation, the two steps are always connected. "The programmers keep going into the designer's office asking for clarifications or making suggestions for changes," says Clark.

Dave Blumenthal agrees. "Design and implementation are very closely tied. No software design is perfect on the first pass. As the implementation begins, the design is revised, and missing pieces are filled in."

Some companies prefer to have projects designed and developed by the same person. Brendan McGinty states, "I recommend that design and development both be done by the same person so that the message isn't muddled in a handoff to someone else."

HARDWARE ENGINEERS ▶▶▶▶▶▶▶▶▷

Software designers and developers may confer with hardware engineers. The hardware engineer determines whether the computer can perform the tasks needed to run the software. The developer and hardware engineer work together to find the best way for the software's code to communicate with the hardware.

SYSTEMS ANALYSTS ▶▶▶▶▶▶▶▶▷

Systems analysts look at computer systems as a whole to see what their needs are. Then they determine how to meet those needs. Many times this involves designing special software. Sometimes in custom software development, the software designer does the systems analysis. It is similar to needs analysis, the first step in the software life cycle.

"Every project has a systems analyst, but often the team doesn't realize it," says Mike Clark. "Someone has to step back a little and look at the project as a whole."

OTHER MEMBERS OF THE TEAM ▶▶▶▶▶

Quality assurance engineers sometimes help test new software to make sure that it functions as designed. Sales and marketing staff promote and sell software. They may also receive feedback from customers and may be able to let the designer know what the customers' needs are.

Once the software is in use, customer support representatives assist people who have trouble using it. Some companies have training departments that offer classes to teach people how to use their software.

These are the people on the software team. Their duties and titles vary depending on the size and type of the project, and the company they work for.

chapter four

WHAT IT TAKES TO BE A SOFTWARE DESIGNER

Creating software involves many related skills. Here are what professionals in the field think are the important talents needed by prospective software designers. Do you possess them? Do you think that you could learn them? This chapter includes questions you can ask yourself to help determine if the field of software design is right for you.

PERSONALITY TRAITS ▸▸▸▸▸▸▸▸

Do you enjoy using logic to solve problems and puzzles? Software designers must be able to think logically. Logical thinking means organizing your thoughts so that one thought leads straight to the next. Though computers work very fast, they really process only one instruction at a time, in the order that those instructions are written. In a sense, logical thinking means training your mind to process information like a computer.

"Design needs to be logical in flow," says Brendan McGinty, "so that the people using the software can focus on the content of the program and not on the navigation."

Logical thinking is also needed to solve problems in software development. Chris Carlson, a software graphics developer with Wolfram Research, explains, "You need to be able to reason backward from the symptoms of wrong behavior to the parts of the program that are causing it."

PAYING ATTENTION TO DETAILS ▶▶▶▶▶▶▶

Do you go through your schoolwork to make sure that the details are correct? Software designers are detail-oriented people. The tiniest mistake—a single incorrect symbol or an out-of-order instruction somewhere within 10 million lines of code—can cause an entire program to malfunction.

"A designer must make sure that all of the objectives of a program are thoroughly covered," says Brendan McGinty.

COMPLEXITY AND PATIENCE ►►►►

If something you do doesn't work, do you try it again in a different way? Do you react calmly to setbacks and difficult problems? Could you learn to work on big, complex programs? Software can be complicated. Chris Carlson says, "I think that one of the hardest lessons to learn in software development is dealing with complexity. Programs can have over one million lines of code—so many that no one person can understand how it all functions."

To develop complicated software, persistence and patience are necessary. Persistence simply means that you keep trying to do something until you find a way that works. Patience is important both in creating and testing software and in working with other members of the software team.

SKILLS ►►►►►►►►

Are you working hard at developing your writing skills? Many software designers are responsible for writing documentation:

the notes, handbooks, and instruction manuals explaining how the program works. According to Brendan McGinty, "Good writing skills are very important in putting together a piece of software. Make your message interesting and clean."

Are you a good listener? Can you express yourself so that others understand you? Communication skills are extremely important. Designers need to communicate with programmers, artists, and other designers. A designer creating custom software must communicate with the client.

Chris Carlson says, "A software designer has to listen well to get a complete picture of a client's needs. He or she also has to communicate the ways in which a program will fulfill those needs and, almost more important, what the program cannot be expected to do."

Rob Walker, a Web page developer with Leo Media, agrees. "If a designer cannot communicate his or her ideas or understand the ideas of another person, valuable production time can be wasted in developing software that doesn't meet the users' needs."

Software designers need good listening skills.

BEING A TEAM PLAYER ▶▶▶▶▶▶▶

Do you work well with others? Being able to work as part of a team is also important. "Most commercial programs are so large and complex that they require the teamwork of many designers and programmers," says Chris Carlson. "In order for the parts of the program to work well together, the designers have to work well together."

BEING A STUDENT FOREVER ▶▶▶▶

Do you like to learn new things? Software designers study hard to keep up with new technology, since software must work on the newest, most advanced computers. Many times, classes and workshops are offered by hardware and software companies to keep their employees' knowledge up-to-date.

"I work for a start-up company," says Dave Blumenthal. "There aren't enough engineers for everyone to do only what he or she already knows how to do. That means that I'm constantly learning new things."

chapter five

PREPARING FOR A CAREER IN SOFTWARE DESIGN

Learning about the field of software design is the first step toward a career in this area. This chapter will tell you how to continue on that path. It covers education, training, and some projects you can try.

JOB REQUIREMENTS ▶▶▶▶▶▶▶▶▶

There are no set requirements for jobs in software design. Employers' needs vary depending on the work to be done. However, since many people want jobs as software designers, it's wise to make yourself as marketable as possible. That means showing employers that you are the best candidate for the job.

HIGH SCHOOL ▶▶▶▶▶▶▶▶▷

You are lucky to be thinking about a career in software design at such a young age. You can take classes in high school that will help you start on the right path. Follow a college preparatory course of study. These are classes recommended for students planning to attend college.

Take advantage of any computer training available in high school.

Try to take classes in computers, science, and English, especially writing, as well as algebra, geometry, calculus, trigonometry, public speaking, and visual art.

"Take an electronics class if you can," Mike Clark recommends. "Understanding something about how hardware works will give you a greater appreciation for what is happening every time you use, program, or design programs for a computer."

Develop good study habits. To get into a good college, you need good grades in high school. Employers prefer candidates with outstanding grades. This shows that the candidate has good work habits and is able to perform well.

FOUR-YEAR COLLEGE DEGREE PROGRAMS ▶▶▶▶

Most four-year colleges offer computer science programs.

Most computer professionals have four-year degrees from a college or university. You will be more marketable if you have a four-year degree.

A degree in computer science will give you training in the development of both hardware and software. Classes include mathematics, programming, electronics, and artificial intelligence. A degree in computer engineering is similar but concentrates more on electronics. Degrees in information systems focus on systems analysis.

COMBINING AREAS OF EXPERTISE

A great way to be marketable is to combine a knowledge of computers with a second area of expertise. Majoring in computer science with a minor in business would make you a perfect choice for an employer looking for a designer of business software. You could also combine computer science with accounting, the physical sciences, education, or graphic

30

design. It is possible to combine almost any four-year college degree with a specialization in computer science.

TWO-YEAR ASSOCIATE DEGREES ▸▸▸▸▸▸

A two-year degree in computer engineering or programming would qualify you for an entry-level programming job. Entry-level programmers, sometimes called technicians, assist software engineers in developing software. They write the actual computer code for portions of programs, and they test software with special equipment. Some junior colleges offer two-year degrees in Web design as well.

GRADUATE DEGREES ▸▸▸▸▸▸▸▸▸▸

There are several reasons to consider going to graduate school after getting a four-year degree. Many jobs are available for people with advanced degrees. Some are in software research and development labs. You might design software that solves advanced mathematical problems or improves the way computer systems operate. Most of these positions are with large companies.

Graduate degrees also offer the opportunity to specialize. Chris Carlson explains, "Because of my interest in computer graphics, I continued on to graduate school so that I could gain an understanding of graphic design. I learned that there are ways of thinking, working, and problem solving that I had gained no inkling of in my engineering education."

INFORMAL TRAINING AND WORK EXPERIENCE ►►►►►►►►

Just as important as a college degree is work experience. Employers want to hire designers with experience. How can you get work experience before you land a job? There are plenty of ways!

Play around on computers. Join a computer club. Find a part-time or summer job in the field. Dave Blumenthal suggests, "Projects like Odyssey of the Mind are excellent. Science fairs are good if you're trying to challenge yourself. Puzzles and games are good; designing them is better. Read a lot, too. That usually works."

Spend the day with a software designer. Experience firsthand what he or she does on the job. Ask your school guidance counselor for help making arrangements.

Try to get access to a computer. Mike Clark says, "Experience is the key. Get a part-time job at a computer store. Use whatever computer resources are available at your school or library."

Rob Walker agrees. "I would suggest taking as much time as you can to learn computers: how they work and how they are utilized. This will provide much insight on software design and what users want in their software programs."

"Most important, start programming," says Chris Carlson. He explains why programming experience is important for a designer: "The difference between a software designer and a programmer is like the difference between an architect and a builder. One makes plans; the other carries them out. Certainly, to be a good architect, you have to understand how buildings are built. Similarly, to be a good software designer, you have to understand how programs are built. Practicing programming and developing good programming habits are the best ways to become a good software designer."

PROJECTS TO TRY ▶▶▶▶▶▶▶▶▶▶

Carlson suggests, "A good way to learn programming is to look at other people's programs and figure out what they do and why. Experiment by making changes. You can find plenty of example programs on the Web, in programming magazines, or in material that is delivered with the programming environment you use on your computer."

Kevin Maxson suggests, "Figure out some small, interesting programming task, and set out to implement it—even something as simple as a tic-tac-toe game."

"If you want to learn how to program, start with an easy language like BASIC," says Brendan McGinty. "Once you are able to write simple programs using BASIC, move up to Visual Basic. From there you can learn Visual C++, and you're on your way. Web page design is pretty easy using tools like FrontPage from Microsoft or PageMill from Adobe. Look at cool Web sites, think of some information you want to present, and create something. Try out all of the different things you can do. Play with it."

Mike Clark suggests the following design project: "Find a second person, like yourself, who is interested in software design. Each of you spend one hour writing out an idea for a computer program. Try to write one page about what functions the program should be able to perform (the specification) and one page with drawings showing how the program should look (the visual design). Don't talk to each other about your projects!

"Now trade your work. Pretend you're the programmer who has to implement the program that the other person designed. Did your partner give you enough information about what to do? Does the program use sound, color, or multi-media? What development tools will you use? What happens if the user clicks in different places with the mouse? What happens when he or she quit the program?

"If the designer did a good job, you could actually program what he or she wanted. If this person did a bad job, you might have created a program that wasn't really what the designer wanted or needed and therefore has to be done over."

chapter six

THE WORKPLACE

With training and experience, you'll be ready to look for a job as a software designer. This chapter will tell you where you might find a job. It describes working conditions and the chances for advancement in the field.

WHERE ARE THE JOBS? ▶▶▶▶▶▶▶▶▶▶

Where would you like to work? You will have many choices. Most software jobs are in computer businesses. Jobs in the business setting pay well but can be unstable, since companies may merge, downsize, or go out of business.

Large corporations such as banks, insurance companies, and real estate businesses all employ software designers. Designers with a background in business and accounting create software for personnel and accounting departments. Government agencies such as the military, the space program, and the Social Security Administration all need software designers. School districts, universities, and hospitals employ software designers, too.

YOUR FIRST JOB ▶▶▶▶▶▶▶▶▶▶

Many people dream of designing computer games like the ones they see in stores. Most of those games are created by large software companies. It is hard to get entry-level design jobs in those companies; most of their designers begin their careers as programmers. After gaining experience and sharing their design ideas, they are promoted into design positions.

It is possible, however, to get an entry-level position designing software for a smaller company. Kevin Maxson says, "Small companies sometimes let developers do their own design. If you are beginning work in a large company like Microsoft or Sun, you will probably be implementing somebody else's design work."

CHANCES FOR ADVANCEMENT ▶▶▶▶

Software designers who have worked for many years may advance to management positions, especially if they are good leaders.

Kevin Maxson is in a leadership position. "I manage a group of seventeen software engineers and also serve as lead software engineer on many projects. In my role as lead software engineer, the lion's share of my time is spent reviewing other engineer's work and suggesting solutions to problems."

Development managers, or project leaders, like Maxson coordinate all aspects of a software project. They decide how the software will be designed and developed. They assign tasks to members of the team. Then they supervise the team as it completes the project.

Many experienced software designers start their own consulting companies. Consultants are hired to work on specific projects. When the project is done, the consultant moves on to another job. Consultants are well paid, but because they must find their own work, their jobs are never stable.

Brendan McGinty shares his experience: "I began my professional career as a software designer/developer. I did my job well and was given the opportunity to manage a small group of other software designers. From there we created software for clients all over the country. We grew our group and made a good reputation for ourselves. After that, I moved up to a higher position that utilized my software design and management skills. That led me to running my own software design and development company."

WORKING CONDITIONS ►►►►►►►►►►

Software designers usually work in an office setting. Many computer companies have a casual work atmosphere. Employees do not wear business suits, except during meetings with clients.

Software professionals generally work forty hours per week. However, most software is developed on a strict schedule. When deadlines are near, work hours increase.

Like many computer professionals, software designers spend lots of time sitting and typing on the computer. This makes them susceptible to eye strain, hand or wrist problems,

and sore backs. There are ways to deal with these problems, such as taking frequent breaks.

Laptop computers and e-mail now make it possible for software designers to work from their homes. Sometimes members of software teams work from different states or countries.

SALARY AND BENEFITS ▶▶▶▶▶▶▶▶▶▶

The salaries earned by software designers vary. Salaries depend on the size and location of the company. Overall, the salary of software designers is much higher than the average for all other industries.

This chart from the National Association of Colleges and Employers shows 1997 starting-salary offers for graduates with four-year degrees in these fields.

Computer programming	$35,167
Information systems	$34,689
Systems analysis and design	$36,261
Software design and development	$39,190
Hardware design and development	$41,237
Master's degree, computer science	$45,853
Ph.D., computer and information science	$61,306

Most designers work for large companies, which offer greater benefits. These include health insurance, vacation and sick time, and a profit-sharing or retirement plan.

EMPLOYMENT OUTLOOK ▶▶▶▶▶▶▶▶

Professor Coddington of the University of Illinois College of Engineering Career Services office states, "Employers now seek more graduates in computer science and computer engineering than we can supply."

As people continue to find new uses for computers and software, jobs will increase. "The tools are going to get easier and yet more sophisticated," says Brendan McGinty. "The computers are going to get faster and more capable. Every field will use software to make people's jobs easier or more efficient, so the potential for employment is endless."

Where is the field of software design heading? In some cases, authoring tools will make programming skills less necessary. However, people with programming skills will still be needed to design and develop authoring tools and many other complex programs. "I would say that good software design skills will retain their importance," says Kevin Maxson.

About the future, Mike Clark says, "Now that people are comfortable with computers, the real revolution will start. You see it in computer shopping and stock trading, in music and book retail. Soon computers will be all over the place. We are on the ramp up to the future."

WORDS.COM: GLOSSARY

applications software Software that is used directly by the computer user.

authoring tools Programs that allow a developer to create software without having to program individual lines of code into the computer.

bugs Mistakes in computer programs.

custom software Software that is developed specifically to meet a client's needs as opposed to being sold in stores.

hardware The physical parts of the computer.

software A word for programs or instruction sets that distinguishes them from the hardware or actual computer equipment.

software life cycle The steps followed in the creation of a program.

specification A document stating the goals of a piece of software and defining ways to reach those goals through design.

systems software Behind-the-scenes software that controls the functions of the computer.

transistors Tiny electronic switching devices used inside computers and other electronic devices.

RESOURCES.COM: WEB SITES AND ASSOCIATIONS

Association for Computing Machinery
http://info.cam.org/

College Board Online
http://www.collegeboard.org

JobProfiles.com
http://www.jobprofiles.com.

Odyssey of the Mind
http://www.odyssey.org

Occupational Handbook
http://www.bls.gov/ocohome.htm

Peterson's Education Center
http://www.petersons.com

Princeton Review Online
http://www.review.com/Birkman

ASSOCIATIONS

American Software Association
c/o ITAA
1616 North Fort Meyer Drive, Suite 1300
Arlington, VA 22209-9998
(703) 522-5055

Association for Computing Machinery (ACM)
1515 Broadway, 17th Floor
New York, NY 10036
(212) 869-7440

Institute for Certification of Computing Professionals (ICCP)
2200 East Devon Avenue, Suite 268
Des Plaines, IL 60018

Microcomputer Software Association
1300 North 17th Street, Number 300
Arlington, VA 22209

Software Publishers Association
1730 M Street NW
Washington, DC 20036
(202) 452-1600

OTHER RESOURCES

List of Camps at Science Service
1719 N Street NW
Washington, DC 20036

OM (Odyssey of the Mind) Association, Inc.
P.O. Box 547
Glassboro, NJ 08028
Phone: (609) 881-1603
Fax: (609) 881-3596

Your local Chamber of Commerce is a great place to look for computer-related internships and jobs.

BOOKS.COM:
FOR FURTHER READING

Burns, Julie Kling. *Opportunities in Computer Systems Careers*. Lincolnwood, IL: VGM Career Horizons, 1996.

Eberts, Marjorie, and Margaret Gisler. *Careers for Computer Buffs*. Lincolnwood, IL: VGM Career Horizons, 1999.

Goldberg, Jan. *Great Jobs for Computer Science Majors*. Lincolnwood, IL: VGM Career Horizons, 1998.

Stair, Lila B. *Careers in Computers*. Lincolnwood, IL: VGM Career Horizons, 1991.

PERIODICALS

IEEE Transactions of Software Engineering
345 E. 47th Street
New York, NY 10017

Software Magazine
Sentry Publishing Inc.
1900 West Park Drive
Westborough, MA 01581

INDEX

A

abacus, 8
applications software, 10

B

Babbage, Charles, 8–9
BASIC, 34
bugs, 15, 16, 19
business software, 10

C

CD-ROM, 6
code, 13, 15, 19, 21
computers, history of, 8–9
custom software, 11, 13, 22, 26
customer support representatives, 22

E

educational software/programs,
     11, 18, 19
ENIAC, 9

F

four year degree, 30, 40

G

graduate degree, 31

H

hardware, 6, 21

I

IBM, 9
implementation, 15, 21

J

junior developers, 14

L

Leibniz, Gottfried Wilhelm, 8
Lovelace, Countess Ada Byron, 8

O

office software, 11
operating systems, 10

P

Pascal, Blaise, 8
programmers, 15, 19–20

Q

quality assurance engineers, 22

R

recreational software, 11

S

software 6, 9, 10, 11, 12, 13, 14, 15–16, 19, 21, 22, 23, 24, 25, 26

    design/designers, 5, 6, 7, 12, 14–15, 23, 24, 25

    development, 5, 7

    industry, 8, 10, 14

    life cycle, 12, 17

    programs, 6

    team, 25, 27

sound, 6, 15

specification, 13, 34

systems analyst, 21

systems software, 10, 20

T

transistors, 9

two year degree, 31

V

Visual Basic, 34

Visual C++, 34

W

Web page developer, 26

48

ABOUT THE AUTHOR

Alice B. McGinty is a therapeutic recreation specialist and a freelance writer of children's books. She lives in Urbana, Illinois with her husband, a software designer, and her two sons.

PHOTO CREDITS

Cover photo © Stephen Simpson/ FPG; pp. 5. 16 © Digital Vision; pp.6 © Thaddeus Harden; pp. 8, 12, 22, 30, 38 © Uniphoto; pp. 11, 18 © Shalhevet Moshe; pp. 21, 29, 37, 39 © Superstock; pp. 25, 27 © International Stock; pp. 26 © Ira Fox; pp. 32, 34 © FPG.

Series Design: Annie O'Donnell

Layout: Rebecca L. Stern

Consulting Editor: Amy Haugesag